Rookie
STAR™
Extraordinary
Animals

Amazing Migrations

Lisa M. Herrington

Content Consultant
Krystina Jarvis
Columbus Zoo and Aquarium, Columbus, Ohio

Reading Consultant
Jeanne M. Clidas, Ph.D.
Reading Specialist

Children's Press®
An Imprint of Scholastic Inc.

Library of Congress Cataloging-in-Publication Data

Names: Herrington, Lisa M., author.
Title: Amazing migrations : Caribou! Elephants! Penguins! / by Lisa M. Herrington.
Description: New York, NY : Children's Press, 2018. | Series: Rookie star. Extraordinary animals | Includes index.
Identifiers: LCCN 2017025796| ISBN 9780531230886 (library binding) | ISBN 9780531233771 (pbk.)
Subjects: LCSH: Animal migration–Juvenile literature.
Classification: LCC QL754 .H47 2018 | DDC 591.56/8–dc23
LC record available at https://lccn.loc.gov/2017025796

Produced by Spooky Cheetah Press
Art direction: Keith Plechaty for kwpCreative, Brenda Jackson for Scholastic
Creative direction: Judith Christ-Lafond for Scholastic

Published in 2019 by Children's Press, an imprint of Scholastic Inc.

Printed in Johor Bahru, Malaysia 108

1 2 3 4 5 6 7 8 9 10 R 28 27 26 25 24 23 22 21 20 19

Scholastic Inc., 557 Broadway, New York, NY 10012.

Photographs ©: cover: Nortbert Wu/Minden Pictures; 1 background: Elenamiv/Shutterstock; 1: Stefan Holm/Dreamstime; 2: Ambientideas/Dreamstime; 3 background: Ingo Arndt/Minden Pictures; 3 top left: Butterfly Hunter/Shutterstock; 3 bottom right and throughout: Marcouliana/Dreamstime; 4-5: Sead Duan/Getty Images; 6-7: 104kelly/iStockphoto; 8-9: Keenpress/National Geographic Creative; 9 inset: Graham Eaton/NPL/Minden Pictures; 10-11: Rene Krekels/NIS/Minden Pictures; 10 inset: Jim McMahon; 11 inset: Joe Petersburger/Getty Images; 12-13: Danita Delimont/Alamy Images; 13 inset: Thomas Kitchin & Victoria Hurst/NHPA/Photoshot/Newscom; 14-15: Paul Nicklin/Getty Images; 15 inset: Stefan Christmann/BIA/Minden Pictures; 16-17: Anup Shah/Minden Pictures; 17 inset: Suzi Eszterhas/Minden Pictures; 18-19: longtaildog/iStockphoto; 19 inset: Colin Monteath/Hedgehog House/Minden Pictures; 20-21: Suzi Eszterhas/Minden Pictures; 21 inset: Mark Carwardine/NPL/Minden Pictures; 22-23: sekarb/iStockphoto; 23 inset: icholas_dale/iStockphoto; 24-25: Minden Pictures/Superstock, Inc.; 25 inset: Michael Pitts/NPL/Minden Pictures; 26-27: Scubazoo/Superstock, Inc.; 27 inset: Steve Winter/Getty Images; 28 top: Rolf Nussbaumer/NPL/Minden Pictures; 28-29 bottom: Jurgen Freund/Nature Picture Library/Getty Images; 28-29 top: Rolf Nussbaumer/NPL/Minden Pictures; 29 top inset: Rolf Nussbaumer/NPL/Minden Pictures; 29 bottom inset: NaturePL/Superstock, Inc.; 30 top left: John L. Absher/Shutterstock; 30 top right: Carol and Mike Werner/Science Source; 30 center left: Richard Herrmann/Minden Pictures; 30 center right: Michael DeYoung/Alaska Stock - Design Pics/Superstock, Inc.; 30 bottom left: Steve Kazlowski / DanitaDelimont.com/Newscom; 30 bottom right: Markus Oblander/imageBROKER/Superstock, Inc.; 31 bottom: Paul Mckenzie/Minden Pictures/Superstock, Inc.; 31 top: Paul Nicklin/Getty Images; 31 center bottom: Suzi Eszterhas/Minden Pictures; 31 center top: sekarb/iStockphoto; 32: Givaga/iStockphoto.

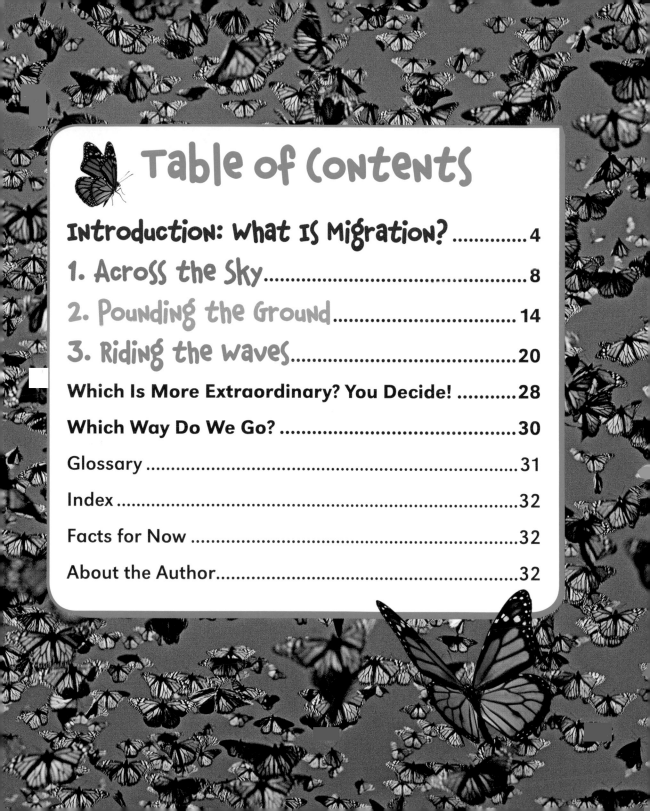

Table of Contents

What Is Migration?

Honk! Honk! These noisy Canada geese are on the move. Where are they going? They are flying south to escape the cold winter. The movement of animals from one region to another is called migration. The Canada geese will return north in summer.

Canada geese fly in a V formation to save energy.

Birds are not the only animals that migrate. Many animals travel great distances. Some migrate to warmer weather. They also travel to

Thirsty elephants migrate to find water.

find food and shelter or to have babies. Animals make incredible journeys by air, land, and sea. Let's look at some of their amazing migrations!

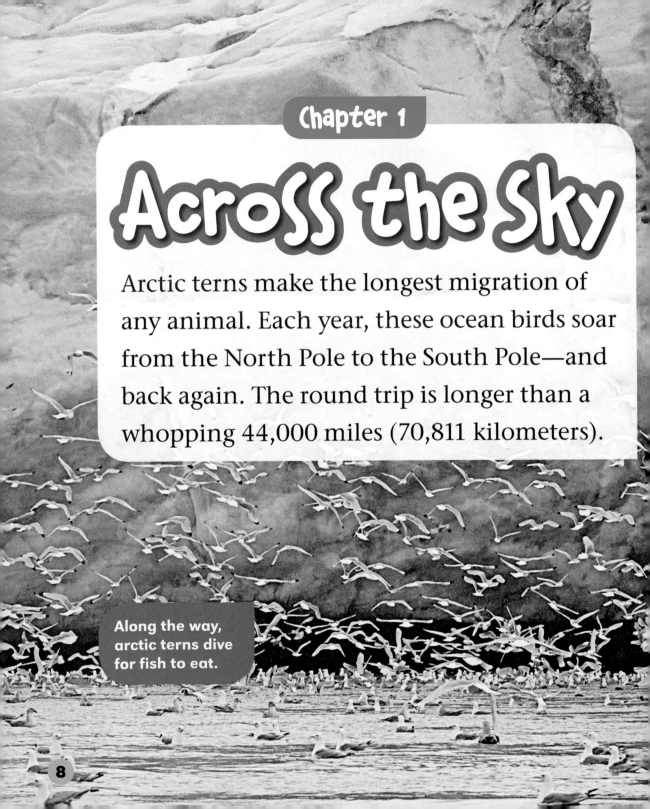

Chapter 1

Across the Sky

Arctic terns make the longest migration of any animal. Each year, these ocean birds soar from the North Pole to the South Pole—and back again. The round trip is longer than a whopping 44,000 miles (70,811 kilometers).

Along the way, arctic terns dive for fish to eat.

During its life, an arctic tern may migrate about 1.5 million miles (2.4 million kilometers). That is like flying to the moon and back three times!

No other insect travels as far as the globe skinner dragonfly. It flies across the ocean from India to Africa. Every year, it covers 11,000 miles (17,703 kilometers) back and forth. That is like traveling across the United States from coast to coast four times! Scientists think these insects are following the rainy season. They need to lay their eggs in pools of water.

Dragonflies are some of the fastest insects. They can zoom at speeds of 34 miles (55 kilometers) per hour. They can fly backward and sideways and can hover like helicopters. They don't even have to stop to eat! A dragonfly snatches an insect right from the air (pictured).

A dragonfly can eat hundreds of mosquitoes in a day.

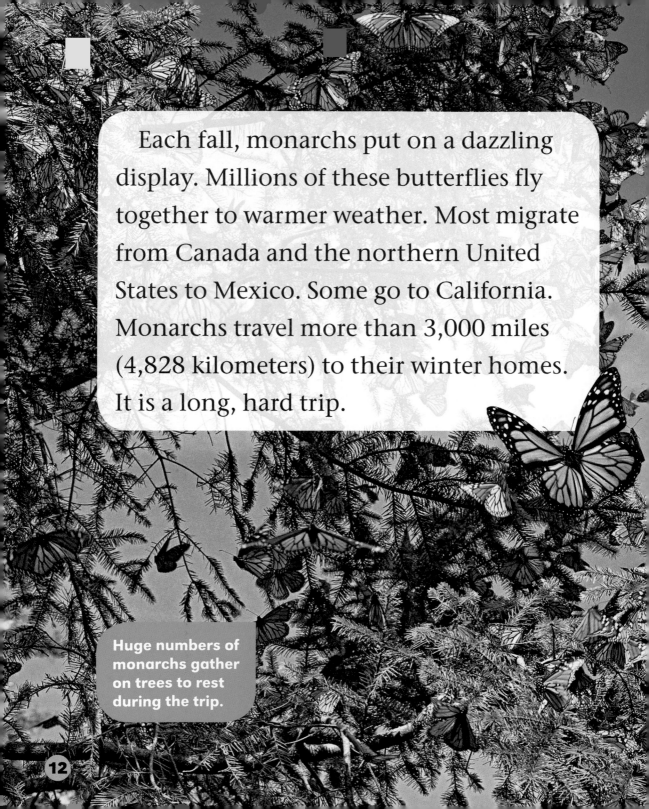

Each fall, monarchs put on a dazzling display. Millions of these butterflies fly together to warmer weather. Most migrate from Canada and the northern United States to Mexico. Some go to California. Monarchs travel more than 3,000 miles (4,828 kilometers) to their winter homes. It is a long, hard trip.

Huge numbers of monarchs gather on trees to rest during the trip.

No one butterfly completes the entire migration alone. It takes many generations to make the round trip. On their return trip north, female butterflies lay eggs on milkweed plants. Then the females die. Their grandchildren and great-grandchildren finish the trip.

eggs

Chapter 2

Pounding the Ground

Imagine walking about 100 miles (161 kilometers) through the South Pole, the coldest place on Earth. Antarctica's emperor penguins do this every year. Each March, whole **colonies** of penguins finish the trip across the ice to reach their nesting grounds. Along the way, they face blinding snowstorms and howling winds.

Penguins are birds, but they cannot fly. They make their migration on foot.

After a female lays an egg, she goes to the ocean for food. The dad holds the egg between his belly and feet for more than two months until it hatches. If the egg touches the icy ground, it will freeze.

egg

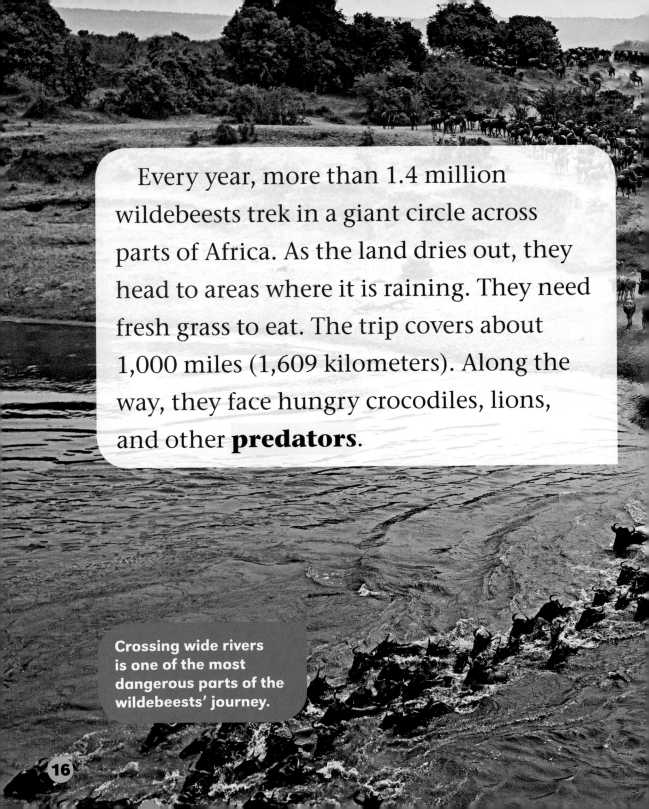

Every year, more than 1.4 million wildebeests trek in a giant circle across parts of Africa. As the land dries out, they head to areas where it is raining. They need fresh grass to eat. The trip covers about 1,000 miles (1,609 kilometers). Along the way, they face hungry crocodiles, lions, and other **predators**.

Crossing wide rivers is one of the most dangerous parts of the wildebeests' journey.

Hundreds of thousands of zebras and gazelles join wildebeests on their massive migration. There is safety in numbers!

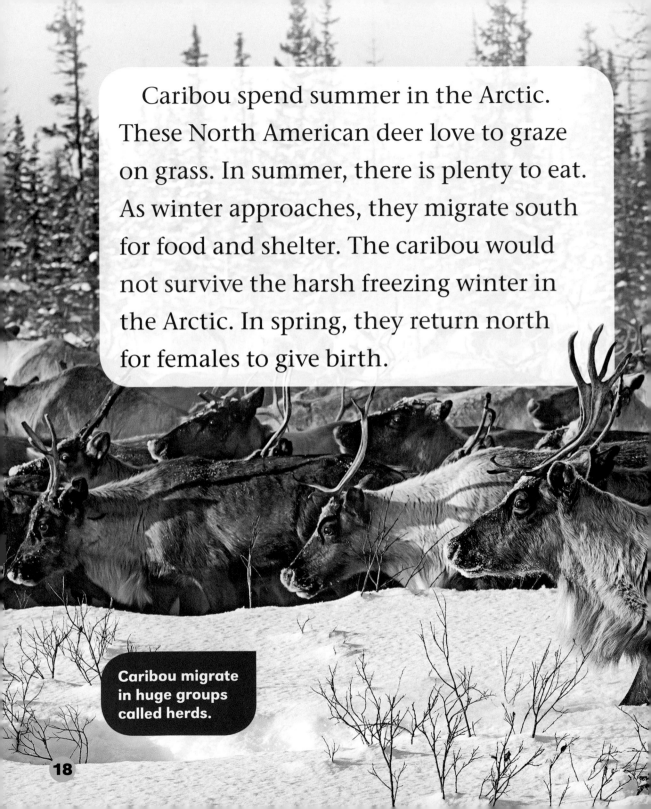

Caribou spend summer in the Arctic. These North American deer love to graze on grass. In summer, there is plenty to eat. As winter approaches, they migrate south for food and shelter. The caribou would not survive the harsh freezing winter in the Arctic. In spring, they return north for females to give birth.

Caribou migrate in huge groups called herds.

Caribou can journey up to 30 miles (48 kilometers) a day. Their large, hairy hooves help them dig through the snow for food. The hooves also act as paddles in water.

Chapter 3

Riding the waves

The gray whale travels the longest distance of any **mammal**. Some swim nearly 7,000 miles (11,265 kilometers) each way. They spend their summers in icy Arctic waters filled with food. As winter approaches, they migrate to warm southern waters near California and Mexico to give birth. Their babies would not survive in the cold waters of the north.

A gray whale is bigger than a bus! This huge mammal migrates for months without eating. So how does it survive on an empty stomach? It stores up a lot of fat for the trip.

People may spot gray whales migrating along the Pacific coast.

Salmon use their amazing jumping ability to swim upstream.

Are these fish flying? No. They are swimming against a strong **current**. Salmon are born in freshwater rivers and streams. Then they migrate to the ocean. When it is time to lay their eggs, the salmon return to the exact streams where they were born! The fish likely use their sense of smell to find their way. During their journey, salmon swim upstream for hundreds of miles.

Brown bears eagerly await the salmon migration. The hungry animals hunt salmon near waterfalls. They catch the leaping fish right in their mouths!

Southern elephant seals are huge animals. Despite their size, they are super swimmers. They migrate almost as far as gray whales. The seals spend about nine months at sea in search of food. In fall, they come ashore to give birth on the rocky beaches of islands near Antarctica. The seals are much bigger than the penguins that share the beach!

A male elephant seal weighs about as much as 100 emperor penguins.

Elephant seals eat almost entirely at sea. They can dive about 1 mile (2 kilometers) deep for their favorite foods—fish and squid. The seals can hold their breath for almost two hours.

penguins

Leatherbacks are powerful swimmers. These sea turtles cover 12,000 miles (19,312 kilometers) each year as they follow ocean highways to look for food. Leatherbacks spend most of their days swimming. Huge front flippers and a streamlined body propel them through the water. Their journey is just one of nature's amazing migrations!

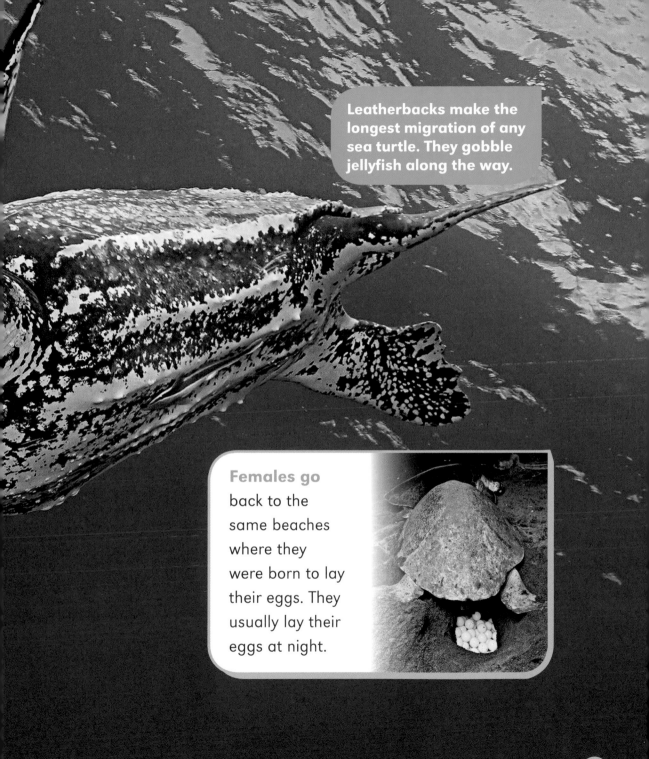

Leatherbacks make the longest migration of any sea turtle. They gobble jellyfish along the way.

Females go back to the same beaches where they were born to lay their eggs. They usually lay their eggs at night.

Which IS More Extraordinary?

Fastest Flappers

Best Group Effort

You Decide!

Get to know two truly amazing travelers and make your own choice.

Ruby-Throated Hummingbirds

- During summer, ruby-throated hummingbirds live in North America.

- Each fall, they embark on a long journey south to Central America.

- They fly nonstop for more than 20 hours across the Gulf of Mexico.

- These tiny birds beat their wings more than 50 times a second!

Red Crabs

- Red crabs live on Australia's Christmas Island.

- Each year, more than 120 million crabs migrate from the island's forest to the coast to give birth.

- As the crabs migrate, the ground looks like a moving red blanket!

- People keep their windows and doors shut during the migration. Good thing it lasts only a few days!

Which Way Do We Go?

Scientists are not sure how migrating animals are able to find their way, but they have some ideas. Based on the clues, can you guess what method each animal below might use?

1

Indigo buntings fly at night.

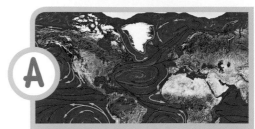

A

Some animals follow ocean currents to find their way.

2

Bluefin tuna migrate in large groups to lay their eggs.

B

Some animals use landmarks on the ground to find their way.

3

Mule deer travel through forests and meadows.

C

Some animals follow the stars to find their way.

ANSWERS: 1 C; 2 A; 3 B

Glossary

colonies (**kah**-luh-nees):
Large groups of animals that
live together.

current (**kur**-uhnt):
The movement of water
in a definite direction in
a river or an ocean.

mammal (**mam**-uhl):
An animal that gives birth
to live young and produces
milk to feed them.

predators (**pred**-uh-turs):
Animals that hunt
other animals for food.

Index

Facts for Now

Visit this Scholastic Web site for more information
on migrations:
www.factsfornow.scholastic.com
Enter the keywords **Amazing Migrations**

About the Author

Lisa M. Herrington has written many children's books about animals. She loves to learn fascinating facts about them. Lisa lives in Connecticut with her husband, Ryan, and daughter, Caroline.